# BASKET RULES

# RULES

*For Kids*

# Author Tony R. Smith

# Basketball Referee Signals

Referee

# Basketball Referee Signals

Beep

Start clock

# Basketball Referee Signals

Beep

Stop clock

# Basketball Referee Signals

Beep

Time-out

# Basketball Referee Signals

Jump Ball

# Basketball Referee Signals

Beep

Substitution

# Basketball Referee Signals

Beckoning

# Basketball Referee Signals

1 Point

# Basketball Referee Signals

2 Point

# Basketball Referee Signals

3 Point

# Basketball Referee Signals

3 Point
(success)

# Basketball Referee Signals

Cancel Score

# Basketball Referee Signals

24 Second
Reset

# Basketball Referee Signals

## Player Foul

# Basketball Referee Signals

Travelling

# Basketball Referee Signals

Technical
Foul

# Basketball Referee Signals

Pushing

# Basketball Referee Signals

Blocking

# Basketball Referee Signals

3-Second
Violation

# Basketball Referee Signals

Intentional
Foul

# Basketball Referee Signals

Control
Foul

Double Foul

# Basketball Players and People Roles

Point
Guard

# Basketball Players and People Roles

BALL
5

Shooting
Guard

# Basketball Players and People Roles

Center
(Big Man)

# Basketball Players and People Roles

BALL

**7**

Power
Forward

# Basketball Players and People Roles

**BALL**

**8**

## Small
## Forward

# Basketball Players and People Roles

Head
Coach

# Basketball Players and People Roles

Reserved Players

# Basketball Players and People Roles

Cheerleader

# Basketball Players and People Roles

Fans

# Time to Draw

# Time to Draw

# Time to Draw

# Time to Draw

# GAME NOTES

_____

_____

_____

_____

_____

_____

# GAME NOTES

_____

_____

_____

_____

_____

_____

# GAME NOTES

_____

_____

_____

_____

_____

# GAME NOTES

_____

_____

_____

_____

_____

# GAME NOTES

# GAME NOTES

# GAME NOTES

_____

_____

_____

_____

_____

# GAME NOTES

_____

_____

_____

_____

_____

# GAME NOTES

_____

_____

_____

_____

_____

_____

# GAME NOTES

_____

_____

_____

_____

_____

_____

# GAME NOTES

---

---

---

---

---

# GAME NOTES

---

---

---

---

---

# GAME NOTES

---

---

---

---

---

---

# GAME NOTES

---

---

---

---

---

---

# GAME NOTES

_____

_____

_____

_____

_____

# GAME NOTES

_____

_____

_____

_____

_____

# GAME NOTES

---

---

---

---

---

# GAME NOTES

---

---

---

---

---

# GAME NOTES

---

---

---

---

---

---

# GAME NOTES

---

---

---

---

---

---

# GAME NOTES

---

---

---

---

---

---

# GAME NOTES

---

---

---

---

---

---

# GAME NOTES

---

---

---

---

---

---

# GAME NOTES

---

---

---

---

---

---

# GAME NOTES

---

---

---

---

---

# GAME NOTES

---

---

---

---

---

# GAME NOTES

---

---

---

---

---

# GAME NOTES

---

---

---

---

---

# GAME NOTES

------

------

------

------

------

------

# GAME NOTES

------

------

------

------

------

------

# GAME NOTES

---

---

---

---

---

# GAME NOTES

---

---

---

---

---

# GAME NOTES

_____

_____

_____

_____

_____

_____

# GAME NOTES

_____

_____

_____

_____

_____

_____

# GAME NOTES

# GAME NOTES

# GAME NOTES

---

---

---

---

---

# GAME NOTES

---

---

---

---

---

# GAME NOTES

# GAME NOTES

Printed in Great Britain
by Amazon

15057941R00038